historic **kent**

a photographic guide

photographed by ben **anker**

written by zoe **anker**

First published in 2006 by
Sutton Publishing Limited · Phoenix Mill
Thrupp · Stroud · Gloucestershire · GL5 2BU

British Library Cataloguing in Publication Data
A catalogue record for this book is available from the British Library.

ISBN 0-7509-4320-3

All information is correct at time of going to print. Locations should be contacted prior to visits to confirm opening times. Some locations have undergone restoration since the photographs were taken. Therefore, some may differ in appearance to those shown.

Typeset in 10.5/18 pt Frutiger
Typesetting and origination by
Sutton Publishing Limited.
Printed and bound in England by
J.H. Haynes & Co. Ltd, Sparkford.

contents

Acknowledgements

We would like to thank each and every person who has helped us see this project through from concept to reality.

One of these invaluable people is Paul Baker, for his original design ideas and imagination.

Our sincere gratitude to Simon Fletcher and Michelle Tilling at Sutton Publishing, and the team who work alongside them, for making a dream come true.

For the superb colour processing throughout this book we must thank the guys at Slater Crosby Photographic, and for the equally exquisite black and white images our thanks to Ricardo da Silva at Keishi.

This book would not have got off the ground without the support of both the National Trust and English Heritage/Sarah Eastell Locations, who allowed us access to some of the most incredible places in Kent. Thanks also to everyone else who allowed us the time and freedom to capture their property in our own style.

Ben would like to make three personal dedications. First to his mum and dad for their everlasting support in helping him to complete a very hard journey. Also to his brother Matt, a legend of a photographer and his inspiration. And finally to Zoe, for her hard work in researching and writing the book – and to apologise for the lost summers.

historic kent

Introduction

One of the most breathtaking views of Kent is from the air during the summer, when infinite shades of green are laid out below you like a beautiful patchwork quilt. Embroidered into that quilt are some of the most imaginative and vibrant gardens in England, often accompanied by a grand stately home. Also scattered across this landscape are castles and other important and spectacular defences. Although their original purpose is no more, they still stand proud, and are maintained as a reminder of the county's history - together with so many other glorious buildings.

All these diverse elements have been captured and documented in many guide books over the years, so in *Historic Kent* we have set out to do something a bit different. This is a contemporary photographic guide to the county, with each image accompanied by a brief description of each location. It's an impressionistic and evocative journey that aims to give the reader a glimpse of Kent's highlights.

The photographs have been organised into a clockwise journey around the county, although there are, of course, some slight diversions. Each group of images is preceded by one of the beautiful landscapes we encountered along the way.

Every image included here has been taken from a position that is accessible to the general public and at a time of day when the locations are open. What you see here is what you will see when you visit - although changes inevitably take place over time. It has obviously not been possible to photograph every beautiful corner of the county, but we hope our selection is representative. We have thoroughly enjoyed rediscovering our home county, and hope that our book will tempt you to discover Kent for yourself.

Ben and Zoe Anker

historic **kent**

one

Cobham Hall
Upnor Castle
Rochester Castle
Rochester Cathedral
The Historic Dockyard
Royal Engineers Museum
Fort Amherst
Mount Ephraim Gardens
Canterbury Castle
Canterbury City Wall & Westgate Towers
Christ Church Gate
Canterbury Cathedral
St Augustine's Abbey
Higham Park
Goodnestone Park
Chillenden Mill

Cobham Hall

The current manor house at Cobham dates from Tudor times and the property has been added to over the years. But there has been a house on this land since the thirteenth century when it came into possession of the de Cobham family. Even more impressive is the land on which the house stood – a staggering 10,000 acres.

The manor and grounds have passed through the hands of several families over the centuries, many of whom were closely affiliated to the Crown. The interior decoration of the hall reflects the grandeur and status of its previous owners, from the seventeenth-century gilt ceiling to the neo-Classical fresco detail on the fireplace surround. In 1962 the house started a new life as a girls' boarding and day school and continues to this day to educate young ladies in the grandest of settings.

Upnor Castle

Upnor Castle is part of a group of naval military fortifications commissioned during the sixteenth century. Overlooking the River Medway, it is a well-preserved castle with few war scars, and has suffered minimal damage over the years.

As the threat of invasion declined at the end of the seventeenth century Upnor became a naval magazine. Today the castle stands as an example of defence before war took to the sky.

12

Rochester Castle

This is every child's image of how a castle should look. Seated on the throne of the Medway towns, Rochester's imposing, sky-scraping Norman castle acted as an impressive defender of the city and maintains a watchful eye over the River Medway.

It is at the centre of year-round activity from Norman re-enactments to a Dickensian street festival, and on warm summer evenings in July the castle plays host to large-scale music events.

Rochester Cathedral

In 2004 Rochester Cathedral celebrated its 1,400th birthday. Considering its age, it's looking good, although that's notwithstanding a bit of remodelling, several facelifts and general essential maintenance work. It is the second oldest cathedral in England: its Saxon roots were put in place in 604 AD, just seven years after St Augustine's arrival in Kent. He appointed Justus Bishop of Rochester in order to promote Christianity on land donated by King Ethelbert. Unfortunately, the building was in a poor state by the time of Bishop Gundulf's arrival in 1077. However, he rebuilt parts of the cathedral and in three years had created a thriving community of Benedictine monks.

During the twelfth century significant areas of the cathedral were destroyed by fires, and general wear and tear has meant that parts have been rebuilt at different periods in various styles. This explains the contradiction of the Gothic-style Quire and the Norman arch over the Great West Door.

Today the cathedral is well used and appreciated all year round, from Sunday services and graduations to popular Christmas carol concerts.

The Historic Dockyard

When a manufacturer announces closure it usually signifies the end of a business. However, after some four centuries of trading in the maritime industry, the Royal Naval Dockyard at Chatham has not chosen retirement. Instead, this most complete naval dockyard from the age of sail has been developed into an educational site, promoting the importance of the production and history of shipping.

On display at the dockyard are many naval vessels, including HMS *Gannet* (1878), HMS *Cavalier* (1944) and the submarine *Ocelot* (1962), which marked the end of warship production at Chatham.

Today the visitor can experience the sights, sounds and smells of the dockyard in 1758 in the Wooden Walls exhibition, and see how the dockyard adapted to the demands of the Navy in peace and at war over the centuries. Without the dockyard, Elizabeth I would have been left shipless against the Spanish Armada, and the Battle of Trafalgar may have had a very different ending had Nelson been without HMS *Victory*.

Royal Engineers Museum

The motto of the Royal Engineers, 'Ubique', translates as 'Everywhere', and this certainly describes the scope and diversity of the collections held at the Royal Engineers Museum. The museum commemorates the personal dedication of those who served with the Corps of the Royal Engineers, and their lives have been thoughtfully represented in a stunning display of memorabilia.

Approximately 30,000 items are held by the museum, including material from the Zulu War in 1879 to personal diaries from the siege at Gibraltar in 1779. The museum, designed by a Royal Engineer in 1904, also looks at the science and technology deployed in wartime, as well as the development and innovation of modern ideas with displays of art, maps and textiles depicting the terrains explored.

The reality of Britain at war is also brought home by the armoured vehicles in the museum grounds, the torpedoes and planes in the courtyard and the medal room, with its twenty-six Victoria Crosses and accompanying photographs of the men who fought and died for their country.

Fort Amherst

Cold and harsh conditions were endured by those stationed at Fort Amherst. Upon entering the 2,500ft of tunnels that burrow 60ft into the chalky hillside, the absence of any natural sunlight creates a swift drop in temperature and the dim electric lighting causes a temporary unbalancing of the senses. As you continue, the design and function of this maze of tunnels, with occasional side passages, steps and the odd open area, becomes more apparent.

The tunnels were begun in 1776 and formed an interlocking part of the fort together with other defensive fortifications built in Medway to protect against intended invasions from France and Germany. The fortifications were never required to defend the country from invasion, so they were used for training exercises until the early twentieth century. During the Second World War the tunnels were occupied by the anti-invasion planning unit as the local Civil Defence Headquarters and remain to this day unmodified, providing one of the best surviving examples of Georgian military architecture.

Mount Ephraim Gardens

While wandering through the extensive gardens at Mount Ephraim you sense a personal touch in the way it has been laid out and maintained, and it is this approach that has been the key to the gardens' success. The gardens were established just before the First World War. From the 1950s they were extended and restored by the then owners, Mary and Bill Dawes, aided by some of their garden enthusiast friends, none of whom were professional gardeners.

The journey around the garden is a whirlwind of striking and imaginative styles, from the oriental-inspired rock garden to the richly scented rose gardens, and yet with all this variety it manages to have a peaceful and tranquil effect on its visitors whatever the season.

Canterbury Castle

Canterbury is recognised across the globe as a significant ecclesiastical city with a fascinating medieval past. The many medieval buildings in the city are complemented by fine Tudor examples to create a unique historical atmosphere. Visitors may meander through the old cobbled streets and see the stunning cathedral, but it seems a shame that many overlook the castle. Originally built shortly after the Battle of Hastings, together with those at Dover and Rochester, Canterbury Castle was constructed as a defence along the route from the coast to London.

The citizens of Canterbury sought protection inside the walled city, which had seven gateways. It was at these manned gateways that the city defended itself. The keep, which dates from the late eleventh to the early twelfth century, was used as a prison for some time from the thirteenth, and continued in that capacity over the next 300 years.

By the early seventeenth century the years of neglect had left the castle in a state of total ruin. It wasn't until 1928 that the City Council acquired Canterbury Castle in order to preserve and restore it. The castle is now a shadow of its former self, but it is loved and appreciated by the residents of Canterbury as part of their city's heritage.

Canterbury City Wall & Westgate Towers

Segments of beautifully landscaped garden rise up to meet the monumental mound to create the Dane John Gardens, which run along part of the City Wall.

Carefully selected trees, shrubs and flowerbeds are enjoyed all year round by the public during lunch hours, days out and local events. Further along the City Wall are the Westgate Towers, which remain a striking entrance into the city and a looming fortification.

Christi Church Gate

Coats of arms, lozenges and shields provide dedications to Christ, royalty and to those who have contributed to the building and restoration of Christ Church Gate. The entrance to the cathedral precinct lived through periods of great upheaval. During the English Civil War Puritan soldiers lassoed the original statue of Christ, pulled it down and destroyed it completely. It was an act that was supported by the Parliament of the time. The original doors were also destroyed, but these were replaced in the 1660s after the restoration of the monarchy. In the nineteenth century it is alleged that the turrets were removed to allow a creditor of the Dean and Chapter a better view of the cathedral clock!

The present gate was built to resemble the one completed in 1517, with the exception of the modern figure of Christ, and provides an inspired and fitting introduction to a cathedral that has had its fair share of drama.

Canterbury Cathedral

Whatever the weather outside, when you walk into the cathedral the atmosphere becomes tangibly different. The familiar but cold stone ecclesiastical architecture is balanced by the warmth within, and regardless of your beliefs the candle-lit, awesome interior of this magnificent building evokes a sense of the spiritual. This sense is heightened by the heavenly music of Evensong.

The cathedral which stands today is the third to have evolved on this site – the previous two having suffered extensive fire damage. St Augustine received the first church from King Ethelbert of Kent in the late sixth century, and over seven years the king and his people were converted to Christianity by St Augustine, who became the first Archbishop of Canterbury. The Romano-British church given to him was little more than a ruin, but it was adapted and extended to meet the needs of the fast-growing religion.

Different archbishops brought with them varying approaches to the post, such as Archbishop Cuthbert, who during his primacy built another church at the east end of the cathedral for the burial of archbishops, believing that an active building, such as St Augustine's Abbey, should be used for the living, not for the dead.

Archbishop Odo inherited a ruinous cathedral and set about its repairs. Replacing the roof took time and the building stood 'open to the sky . . . yet did not rain fall that would impede the clergy in the performance of their duty or restrain the people from coming'. Unfortunately, the Norman Conquest of 1066 hit the city hard and the cathedral was devastated by fire a year later.

One incident that shook the cathedral to its very foundations and firmly placed it on the map as a destination for pilgrimage was the murder of Archbishop Thomas Becket on 29 December 1170. Four knights, William de Tracy, Reginald Fitzurse, Richard le Breton and Hugh de Morville, made haste to Canterbury, believing that they were on a quest to serve their king. They entered the cathedral where there was a quarrel with Becket, who then calmly met his end at their hands. Becket, the martyr, was hailed a saint. The king, Henry II, felt great remorse and feared divine retribution.

On a summer's day in 1174 the king paid his penance before the citizens of Canterbury, walking barefoot from St Dunstan's Church to the cathedral. There he knelt at the marble tomb of Thomas Becket and received 'monastical beats' in the name of Christ. He spent the night in the cathedral in prayer before returning to London the next day. Only a few months later a fire swept the cathedral, devastating it once again.

Over the years the cathedral has survived relatively unscathed. During the Second World War the building was undamaged, although Canterbury was bombed – prompting a visit from George VI and his family to celebrate its survival.

The traditions of the cathedral still apply today with it playing host to special events and regular daily services. It stands amid a developing city while its people and visitors from afar flock to it, seeking the peace, solitude and time for reflection that this beautiful, majestic and significant building provides.

34

St Augustine's Abbey

St Augustine's Abbey has had a tempestuous affair with the property market. It has made a number of transitions, from a burial site to a monastery to a Royal Palace. It escaped destruction during the Viking invasions and has been demolished, reconstructed, expanded and extended over a period of approximately 1,400 years.

Originally the Abbey of St Peter and St Paul, the site was developed by St Augustine and the King of Kent to create a home for the increasing number of Roman monks assisting in the evangelisation of Canterbury. The abbey prospered as a place of intellectual and theological brilliance. It was renamed St Augustine's Abbey by Archbishop Dunstan in the tenth century.

36

Higham Park

Higham Park is a superb example of personal achievement. The grounds and property were purchased by two cousins in 1995, who since then have made significant personal sacrifices to restore the estate to how it would have looked when it was ceded to the De Hegham family by Edward II. The cousins experienced ferocious bidding and lengthy negotiations before purchasing the property, the selling particulars of which would have included broken windows, cracked and holed ceilings, water running where it should not and honey running from the bees' nest in the chimney if you lit a fire.

Now, after Higham Park's extensive restoration, the particulars would highlight the eighteenth-century Palladian frontage, the eighty-seven rooms, the coach house, the completely renovated interior, the sunken Italian garden and the terraced rose garden, all of which make the former headquarters of the Army during the Second World War a welcoming home for the cousins, as well as a fascinating illustration of their dedication.

Goodnestone Park

Many great ancestral homes and estates across Britain have been divided or abandoned because of war, lack of an heir or the hefty finances required to maintain a large property. In a rural pocket of Kent lies the home and park garden of the FitzWalter-Plumptre family. Goodnestone Park has been Lord FitzWalter's family home for over 300 years, and there are reminders of this not only inside the house but also in the gardens. Even the village pub is appropriately named the FitzWalter Arms.

In the gardens there is a magnificent avenue of limes, which was planted to celebrate family birthdays and betrothals. The thick, entwined, deep-rooted Cedar of Lebanon planted in about 1704 has been at Goodnestone for as long as the FitzWalters.

Chillenden Mill

Dotted throughout Kent are small parishes far from the busy town centres and motorways. The village of Chillenden, with its ninety-four residents, pub, church and village hall, enjoys the peace and tranquillity that the Kentish landscape has to offer. Until 2003 it was the home of Chillenden Mill, one of east Kent's historic landmarks and one of only four Kentish post mills.

The mill was destroyed during a storm which left it all but a pile of shattered wood. After extensive television and newspaper coverage and support from the district and parish councils, the mill has been restored to its former glory by Kent County Council. A few modifications have been made to ensure its future stability and it can once again be enjoyed and appreciated as a reminder of Kent's former milling industry.

two

historic **kent**

Whitstable

Famous for its fresh fish, and in particular its oysters, Whitstable has remained a busy fishing port with boats of all shapes and sizes lining the water's edge. However, the once-sleepy town centre is not so sleepy any more.

Whether it is the white weather-board housing, laid back atmosphere or bracing sea air, in recent years Whitstable has become a hive of bohemian activity from art galleries and specialist delicatessens to the Horsebridge Centre for comedy nights. It is a seasonal retreat for Londoners, and, yes, you will bump into the odd celebrity, but you cannot escape the friendly feeling of community among its residents and local businesses.

Whitstable Castle

Whitstable Castle, despite its name, was never built as a defensive structure. Dating from 1790, it was originally constructed as a house for a local businessman.

Various modifications over the years have produced the building that can be seen today, which is used by the local community for various activities. The gardens, which command impressive views across the sea, are open to the public and provide a respite from the hustle and bustle of this busy fishing town.

Reculver Towers

The Romans enjoyed their home comforts – beautiful bathhouses, sunny weather, good wine and food – so it would not have been agreeable for a soldier from Rome to be posted to Britain.

The Roman Empire had swiftly occupied much of Europe, and Britain, which was not unified under one ruler, was a desirable conquest. In 43 AD Reculver was used as a camp by the invading Romans sent by Claudius. Excavations of the area have found that the local Roman fort had a bathhouse. Italian spring vegetables planted by the Romans continue to grow wild around the site.

The fort was abandoned in the mid-fourth century, but it did not become a church until the foundations were put in place in 669 AD. Over the centuries St Mary's Church evolved, and its structure was altered and expanded until, unfortunately, erosion from the sea got the better of it. With a number of buildings in the area facing a similar fate, the parishioners agreed to its destruction in 1809, building a new church further inland.

Reculver's signature twelfth-century twin towers remain a familiar landmark. Originally built to mark the coastline for nearby ships, they are now an important historical reminder of Kent's diverse history.

Botany Bay

This is simply one of the most stunning stretches of water the south-east has to offer. In the summer windbreaks of all colours furnish the coastline as families enjoy picnics filled with sand and parents juggle ice creams for hungry children.

Situated in the smuggling town of Broadstairs, this golden beach provides children with the perfect location to play pirates and explore for treasures.

Bleak House

Few buildings receive the accolade of being the inspiration for a book written by one of our greatest novelists.

Charles Dickens certainly regarded Bleak House in the seaside town of Broadstairs with immense affection, as he and his family spent most summers living in it. Breathtaking views across the bay from Bleak House are just as inspirational today.

Kingsgate Bay

The Isle of Thanet boasts 26 miles of coastline with fifteen sandy bays and beaches. The Viking Coastal trail links Reculver in the north to Pegwell Bay in the south and provides an assortment of terrains for walkers and cyclists. The variety of beaches caters for all, from the traditional bucket and spade beach with Punch and Judy through to those ideal for wind and kite surfing, and others that provide an opportunity to experience the nature reserves with seals, turnstones, chalk reefs and rock pools.

Kingsgate Bay enjoys a peaceful existence, but the caves in the chalky cliffs point to a darker and more sinister past. It was a landing point for smugglers and pirates, who braved the crashing waves under the moonlight before venturing into the nearest towns and villages.

St Augustine's Cross

It was just another day in the spring of 597 AD when St Augustine made the final leg of his journey to England and landed on the Isle of Thanet.

Travelling from Rome and sent with the blessings of Pope Gregory the Great, St Augustine had arrived, no doubt with immense anticipation, to spread the word of Christ. The cross is said to be located where he landed and started his mission by holding a mass.

AUGUSTINUS
AD RUTUPINA LITTORA ...

Richborough Roman Fort

A combination of vision and imagination enables the ruins at Richborough to become the busy town and port it once was following the Roman invasion in 43 AD. Initially built as a fort and remaining as a base camp from which the occupation could progress, the site developed into a town during a period of peace from 60 AD to 85 AD. Roads, dwellings and an amphitheatre were built, but it was the completion of a monumental arch that provided a political statement at the centre of the town which greeted visitors from across the channel.

In the third century the town was under threat of Saxon invasion. The earth fortifications were replaced with the vast walls that can be seen today, which enclose an area of 8 acres; however, much of the central town was demolished. Fortunately, excavation has unearthed a huge number of Roman artefacts, some of which can be seen at the museum on site and some of which are displayed at the British Museum. They provide a detailed history of passing life and trade at Richborough.

Sarre Windmill

Sarre Windmill is Kent's last working commercial windmill and one of the few still operating in Britain.

Built in 1820 by Canterbury millwright John Holman, the mill operated by wind power with a steam engine until 1922 when the sails were removed and a gas engine was installed. Trading stopped between the First and Second World Wars, when it was used as an observation post, and thereafter the mill was boarded up and left to deteriorate.

In the mid-1980s the mill was purchased by Malcolm Hobbs and a restoration project was begun. Much of the timber used to restore the mill came from early nineteenth-century buildings that had been demolished at Chatham Dockyard, the gas engine was repaired, and in 1991 the mill was reopened, selling stone-ground flours that continue to be manufactured to this day.

Deal Castle

The castle's squat, thick design meant that it could handle a heavy attack and its height enabled gun ports with an all-round artillery coverage to be sited there. The main keep sits on six cylindrical bastions which, in turn, sit on six larger bastions. From overhead, this creates a shape possibly influenced by the Tudor Rose. The basement houses The Rounds, a network of tunnels which provides a comprehensive system of communication to all gun ports to warn of imminent attack.

Architecturally speaking, Deal Castle has that functionality of design so beloved of the twentieth century, concentrating on function rather than frippery. It was meticulously planned and speedily constructed to provide a practical solution to the threat of war, and all this from the showy and extravagant Tudor king, Henry VIII.

Walmer Castle

Walmer Castle was originally built in Tudor times as a coastal defence because of persistent threats from Catholic Spain. It was thereafter transformed into an elegant home and is the official residence of the Lord Warden of Cinque Ports – for twenty-three years the Duke of Wellington fondly held the position until he passed away within the castle walls.

The gardens of Walmer Castle boast flower beds bursting with the colours and aromas associated with a country garden. They contrast strikingly with the sea and castle moat, which has been developed into a garden feature.

St Margaret's Bay

It all began 450,000 years ago, when the North Sea was a huge sheet of ice and Britain was joined to France by a land bridge of chalk. As the temperature began to rise, so did the water levels with rivers swelling and the North Sea melting. The land that joined Britain to the rest of Europe acted like a dam which eventually gave way, and the flowing waters cut a channel through the north tip of the continent creating the white cliffs.

Tucked away at the bottom of a winding road, the bay of the village of St Margaret's-at-Cliffe has seen a varied history. An attempt to stop smuggling was made by the government in 1757; ships were grounded, wrecked and cargo was looted in the nineteenth century; the area suffered bomb damage during the First and Second World Wars, with complete evacuations save for the troops; and more recently there has been a different kind of battle for land preservation to fight off potential development. Today the bay is an area of natural beauty with scenic walks, quiet skies, wild flowers, cream teas and a peaceful shoreline.

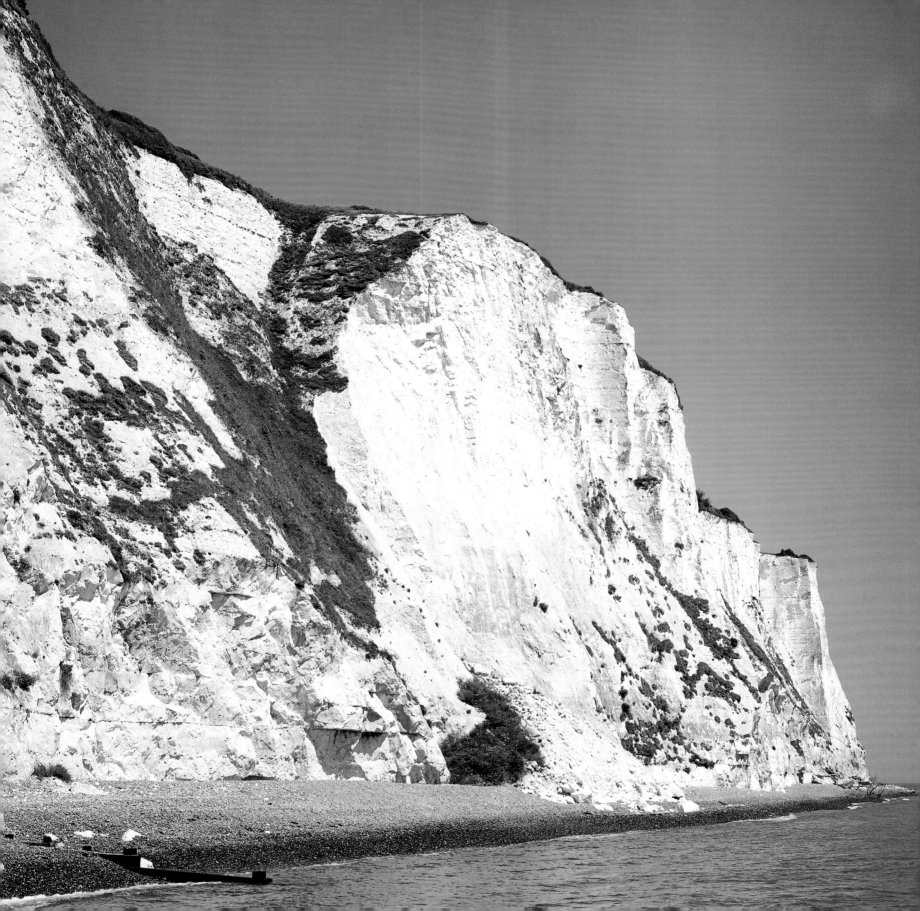

Dover Castle

Described as the Key of England, since the twelfth century Dover Castle has been a significant military centre of activity.

Both Henry VIII and Churchill attended to matters of business within its walls; in the depths of the cliffs below the castle the finer details of the retreat from Dunkirk were outlined in May 1940. As recently as the Cold War this great defence would have accommodated the regional seat of government had there been a nuclear attack. What this castle lacks in grace it makes up for in presence and location.

South Foreland Lighthouse

On a clear day some of the best views across to France can be appreciated on the walk from the entrance of the Gateway to the White Cliffs Visitor Centre to South Foreland Lighthouse. The pathways take the windy route to the lighthouse, providing the seascape views as well as glimpses of the sheer chalky cliff faces to the waters below.

The 69ft tower provided a warning light to mariners approaching the treacherous Goodwin Sands, and Marconi used it to make the first ship-to-shore transmission on Christmas Eve in 1898. The lighthouse was also central to events the following year when the first wireless message was sent across the channel.

Battle of Britain Memorial

On 10 July 1940 a battle began in the skies above Kent that continued through the summer and into the autumn, marking a turning point in the Second World War. The Battle of Britain was the last major conflict over British soil and was a victory which cost the lives of more than 500 Allied aircrew.

On the cliffs at Capel-le-Ferne, at a location known in 1940 as Hellfire Corner, stands the national memorial to those who lost their lives. It was unveiled by Her Majesty Queen Elizabeth the Queen Mother in 1993 and was the first permanent monument to those who fought in the Battle of Britain. From the air, the memorial is in the shape of a three-bladed propeller, and at its centre on the propeller-boss sits a lone pilot watching over the sea. This memorial, sculpted by Harry Gray, is a continuous reminder of the brave aircrews who fought for Britain and represents the pride and respect felt by its people.

three

Chilham

The area around the delightful village of Chilham is ideal for walks and for taking in the vast green patchwork of the Kentish landscape. In the village itself a privately owned castle sits behind an entrance on the small square, which is surrounded by cottages, church, tea room, pub and shop, and which also plays host to a hugely popular May Fayre.

The French Mill, built in the late nineteenth century, is a stone's throw from Chilham Lake, which has become a popular fishing location and is home to some magnificent swans. Like Whitstable, Chilham's reputation has drawn in visitors from afar and it has become a sought-after location in which to settle; however, this has not marred the character of the village.

Beech Court Gardens

As the Garden of England, Kent is under a degree of pressure to maintain its reputation and Beech Court Gardens doesn't disappoint.

It is a beautiful example of how working to create a garden around the natural contours of the land can give spectacular results and preserve the existing wildlife. Year-round colour and scents provided by both flowers and trees make this an ideal location to take in the ancient Kentish countryside.

Eastwell Manor

A significant factor in the development of Eastwell Manor has been its dependence on a continuous flow of residents and visitors. The estate has passed through the hands of several owners over the years and now seems to have found its niche as a successful country house hotel. The very building seems to flourish when it is full of wedding parties, conferences and dinner guests.

Whatever the season, Eastwell tempts and beguiles. During the summer the vast lawn plays host to croquet matches as guests linger on the terrace sipping their Pimms and soaking up views of the surrounding countryside. In the winter visitors snuggle into the fat leather armchairs dotted around the building in front of large open fires, enjoying sumptuous trays of tea and scones. It is, however, at Christmas that Eastwell looks its finest, with the most extravagant Christmas trees, the snow-tipped topiary and the smell of mulled wine. This is a luxurious Kentish hideaway.

Smallhythe Place

Affectionately nicknamed The Farm, Smallhythe is an example of exceptional Tudor architecture. The attractive, heavily beamed property caught the attention of the prominent Victorian actress Ellen Terry, who fulfilled her desire to live out her life there 'as a dear old frump in an armchair'.

Terry achieved international acclaim as a serious Shakespearean actress, with audiences quickly recognising her ability to effectively 'become' Ophelia, Lady Macbeth and many others at the Lyceum Theatre in London. The costume room at Smallhythe honours this and houses a marvellous collection of her costumes. In fact, the whole house is filled with a sense of nostalgia for a career and life on stage, with theatrical make-up and jewellery among family photographs: Smallhythe was fondly preserved by Terry's daughter. Today, performances in the Tudor barn continue to keep alive the memory of Ellen Terry.

Sissinghurst Castle Garden

The impressive tower, built in the mid-sixteenth century, shows the grandeur of this Elizabethan 'castle', which was built on the site of a thirteenth-century manor house.

The manor of Sissinghurst was owned by the Baker family throughout the fifteenth and sixteenth centuries. Members of the family were responsible for building the Elizabethan mansion and tower, the remains of which are seen today. The Bakers, a well-connected and wealthy family, enjoyed entertaining royalty during their time at Sissinghurst. Unfortunately, the castle fell into serious decline and was neglected for many years; it was even used as a prison for a short spell in the mid-eighteenth century. It was not until 1930 when Vita Sackville-West and her husband Harold Nicolson purchased the property that redevelopment began. Time, money and a considerable passion have rescued this now glorious home and garden.

Bedgebury Pinetum

Generally we get our bearings by a swift analysis of familiar surroundings, including landscape, climate, scent and many other contributory factors. However, even the most intrepid and experienced rambler would be forgiven for getting lost in Bedgebury Pinetum.

With over 6,000 trees, Bedgebury offers a unique opportunity to walk through peaceful Kentish countryside while at the same time being transported to the Orient as we walk through the Japanese and Chinese Glades, and then to California, as we pass under the towering Redwoods.

Scotney Castle Garden & Estate

Reflections of the castle in the moat are one of the most enchanting features of the Scotney Castle Estate. The romantic fourteenth-century castle is surrounded by shadows of a picturesque ruin and fairytale gardens.

From the entrance to the estate you look down to the magnificent 770-acre grounds where the old castle stands. The unique gardens are laid out as neatly cut lawns and meadowland. Do not be fooled by the natural look of the meadow: as a Site of Special Scientific Interest (SSSI) and home to the rare green-winged orchid, it is just as carefully maintained as the lawn.

Bayham Old Abbey

Originally founded in the thirteenth century, the abbey was a casualty of the Reformation and Dissolution in the sixteenth century and then subject to some restoration in the eighteenth. It is now a ruin. As with any building of such age, Bayham Old Abbey has lived through some of the most destructive, volatile and inventive periods of English history, but probably one of the reasons that anything of it remains is down to its secluded and peaceful location. This was well suited to its original residents, who were Premonstratensian canons, devoted to St Augustine.

Unfortunately, no building is free from financial upheavals, ever-changing politics and the elements, but the care and conservation undertaken by the current owners has ensured that some quite beautiful, elegant architectural features remain of this once-active Kentish abbey.

Groombridge Place Gardens

These gardens succeed where many locations fail in being a truly captivating and stimulating day out for children and their parents.

For the adults, the handsome grounds bloom all year round with explosions of buttery daffodils in spring and the fiery dahlias which cover the ground in the autumn. The tranquil, majestic backdrop of the seventeenth-century manor house transports visitors to a different era while they meander among the resident peacocks. Meanwhile, in the Enchanted Forest, children's imaginations run riot on the giant swings, in the Serpents' Lair and on the Dark Walk.

94

The Church of King Charles the Martyr

Tunbridge Wells has grown to its present state from humble beginnings. Not even marked on seventeeth-century maps, it has become a prominent and thriving commercial town and spa. The man who recognised its potential was Thomas Neale, a seventeenth-century entrepreneur who saw the location and the unique natural spring flowing into the area as an opportunity. The area of the springs is now known as The Pantiles and forms the centrepiece of Tunbridge Wells.

The Church of King Charles the Martyr is the oldest building in Tunbridge Wells and has been repeatedly extended to cope with the expansion of the town. The town itself had become a popular spa resort by the late seventeenth century, and some visitors split their time between Bath and Tunbridge Wells. It was the place to be seen. Wealthy visitors strolled down The Pantiles (adhering to strict rules that separated the gentry from the poor) and enjoyed the spring's health-giving properties.

And it was not just the gentry who enjoyed the beauty of Tunbridge Wells; royalty has often visited the town over the years. A young and pious Princess Victoria prayed with her mother in the King Charles church, and in the early twentieth century her son, King Edward VII, awarded the town its title Royal Tunbridge Wells. It has kept its place as a prestigious and attractive town to visit. It is a testimony to Thomas Neale's vision.

Dunorlan Park

Donorlan Park in Tunbridge Wells is one of many parks in Kent and, like several others, it was once the private grounds of a very large mansion. The property, built in the mid-nineteenth century, no longer exists.

The grounds remain and are, with the completion of a major Heritage Lottery Fund restoration in 2005, one of the best-preserved examples of work by renowned Victorian landscape gardener Robert Marnock. Henry Reed, the owner of the mansion and garden, was a committed evangelical and William Booth, founder of the Salvation Army, held missions on the lawns at Dunorlan. An avenue of cedar trees links a fountain to a Grecian Temple, a lake and a cascade: with such variety, a walk around this Grade II listed park is a fine way to spend a summer's day.

Hop Farm Country Park

Oast cowls are scattered throughout Kent and are familiar sights on the skyline. It is believed that the commercial cultivation of hops for beer brewing began in Kent in the sixteenth century and the hop farm was influential in providing a trade that continues in the county today. Over the centuries the beginning of September would see a flurry of activity on all hop farms as tens of thousands of visitors from outside the county came to enjoy annual working holidays.

Oast houses were designed for the drying of hops. At the Hop Farm this was done in its impressive collection of traditional buildings until 1984. Today, the Hop Farm is a living museum, providing a detailed insight into a well-known Kentish tradition, where visitors can find out about an industry that was vital to the economy of the county.

Tonbridge Castle

The land on which Tonbridge Castle stood was a gift from William the Conqueror to one of his most devoted and loyal noblemen, Richard Fitzgilbert.

The original mud and timber castle built on this land was destroyed twenty years later in a battle against the Conqueror's successor, William Rufus, but the land remained in the Fitzgilbert family. In the thirteenth century a stone castle was built on the site. The motte and bailey gatehouse which still remains is surrounded by 14 acres of open land and gardens overlooking the River Medway.

four

historic kent

Leeds Castle

On land just outside Maidstone there has been a dwelling with the name Leeds for over 1,000 years. It has had over sixty owners, been home to six medieval queens and a palace to a king. It is packed with paintings, tapestries, armour, furniture, books, china, glass, ceramic birds and even houses a dog collar museum!

Perhaps the most fabulous reminders of the royal presence are the queen's rooms. One queen who lived in the castle was Catherine de Valois, wife of Henry V. After he died she married Owen Tudor. Their son Edmund was father of Henry VII, the first Tudor monarch. Her chamber was a place in which to greet, converse with and entertain courtiers and petitioners rather than to sleep. It would have been a busy and active room with many visitors, and its luxurious decor indicated wealth and stability.

Naturally, as with many properties in Kent, Henry VIII owned the castle during his reign, and a portrait of the man himself towers over the sixteenth-century stone carved fireplace in the banqueting hall.

His son, Edward VI, gave the castle to Sir Anthony St Leger, Lord Deputy of Ireland. It then passed to other notable families such as the Culpepers, the Fairfaxes and the Wykeham Martins.

In 1926 Leeds Castle was purchased by the Hon. Mrs Wilson Filmer, who later became the Hon. Olive, Lady Baillie. She devoted herself to the restoration of Leeds Castle aided by her impeccable taste and eye for detail. She was the heart of the castle, occupying it for longer than any of her predecessors.

Since Lady Baillie's death in 1974 the property has been run by the Leeds Castle Foundation, but her presence is still evident in every painting she hung and even in details, such as the castle's black swan monogrammed towels in her bathroom.

Stoneacre

An attractive garden and a house of Yeoman-farmer design make Stoneacre a popular location for artists as well as tourists. Today its curators keep alive a home that has been occupied since the late fifteenth century.

The house was allowed to fall into a state of disrepair after the First World War, and what we see today is the result of the dedication of one man to carefully restore it to its pre-1914 glory. Aymer Valance worked tirelessly to recreate an interior and exterior that would have been the pride of anyone in medieval Britain, while the garden and terraced courtyard have been developed to complement the house all year round.

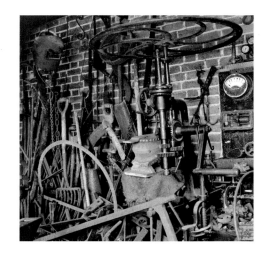

Museum of Kent Life

Scrumping, hopping and farming are all part of Kentish life, and these traditions are on display at the Museum of Kent Life, near Maidstone. It is a truly fascinating glimpse of some of the county's most significant elements and explores its history. Much of its focus is on Kentish industries, such as hopping, which was big business for the area, creating jobs in Kent and in the surrounding counties and south-east London.

The signature cowls of an oast house look glorious in the lush patchwork landscapes of the county; this museum gives us an insight into their function. A good climate and a healthy soil make Kent an ideal location for farming, which has always been a major industry in the county. The museum shows not only life on the land – the heavy toil that this involved as well as the nostalgic scenes of sunshine and haymaking – but also the importance of trade. There have been many changes over the centuries, including mechanisation that has so significantly reduced the number of agricultural workers, the increasing importance of organic crops, and even changing climate patterns, but has Kentish life really changed that much?

112

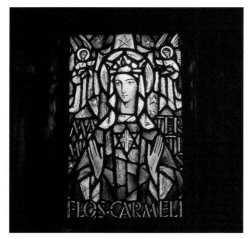

The Friars

The friars at Aylesford successfully combine the peace and solace of prayer with work in a vibrant and thriving community. The Friars – Aylesford Priory – is part of the Order of Carmelites and was established in the mid-thirteenth century. It continues today with the same beliefs and traditions.

One of these traditions is that the friars work in the wider community, for example in schools, the neighbouring prison and at local events. The priory itself is in a tranquil and reverent setting, and the stunning ceramic and sculpted shrine of Our Lady of the Assumption touches the hearts of over 250,000 visitors every year.

St Leonard's Tower

The current inhabitants of St Leonard's Tower, some of our fine feathered friends, enjoy a secluded and peaceful existence, taking in the surrounding landscape and nesting in the Kentish ragstone rubble.

But little do they know of the conflicts of opinion between experts as to who built the tower. There are strong similarities between the tower at St Leonard's and that at Rochester, suggesting that Gundulf, a former Bishop of Rochester, was the architect. It is clear, though, that the tower had both domestic and defensive functions, and had a variety of uses over the years.

Coldrum Long Barrow

4.32 am, 21 June – the summer solstice. As many gather to watch the sunrise at Stonehenge, those of us in Kent have the opportunity to take the shorter journey to the standing stones at Coldrum to enjoy the gradual illumination of the Medway Valley while also taking time out for peaceful reflection and meditation.

Dating from the Neolithic period (4,000 to 3,000 BC), long barrows were burial chambers and also places of religious worship. The stones at the Coldrum site are reputed to be older that those at Stonehenge. The barrow has partially collapsed, but it is still the best example of a tomb in Kent. Visitors and druids alike can make offerings to the wishing tree, before heading off to the local village of Trottiscliffe for lunch.

Great Comp Garden

Situated in the grounds of a Tudor house, Great Comp is a marvellous example of how a garden can be created and developed without experience but with equal enthusiasm and hard work.

Since 1957 Roderick and Joy Cameron have extended the garden to 7 acres from its original 4½ acres. Rather than sitting down and planning each area of the garden square foot by square foot, they decided to start with a basic idea and develop it from there. A key feature was that there should be year-round colour and it was also designed so that the various areas respond to the changing seasons, to provide visitors with a diverse and interesting tour. It is a vision that has been successfully achieved.

Old Soar Manor

Nestling in the Bourne Valley is Old Soar Manor, a fine example of a late thirteenth-century medieval knight's manor house.

Its design was meticulously thought out and combines homely features, such as a first-floor solar living chamber, a chapel and a large garderobe, with those necessary for defence against would-be thieves and invaders.

Ightham Mote

Ightham Mote has been subject to architectural development for over 500 years, but none more important than that undertaken in recent times. A fourteenth-century manor house, this Grade I listed building and scheduled ancient monument provides a stunning centrepiece to the medieval garden and peaceful moat.

A £10 million restoration of the house has recently been completed. The building was taken apart, measured, photographed and recorded with numerous discoveries being made along the way, allowing further rooms to be opened to the public. Ightham Mote was described by Nikolaus Pevsner as 'the most complete small medieval manor house in the country', and this is going to be the case for many more hundreds of years thanks to the restoration.

Knole

Observing the beautiful deer that live and graze peacefully in the shadows of the glorious medieval façade of Knole, the visitor can appreciate why Henry VIII just had to have it, forcing Thomas Cranmer to give the house to him in 1538. Knole's contents reflect the grandeur of the architecture with examples of some of the finest Stuart furniture, paintings by Gainsborough and an elaborately crafted staircase.

Knole was originally built as an ecclesiastical palace for Thomas Bourchier, Archbishop of Canterbury. Elizabeth I presented it to her cousin Thomas Sackville in 1566 and his descendants continue to live there to this day.

Penshurst Place & Gardens

To have served several Tudor and Stuart monarchs and to keep your head was quite an achievement. The Sidney family, owners of Penshurst Place since 1552, enjoyed just such lengthy service. The house and gardens continue to this day to provide the Sidney family with a comfortable home and luxurious surroundings in which to entertain.

Penshurst's original owner was Sir Stephen de Penchester, a distinguished royal servant whose tomb can be seen in Penshurst church. Subsequently it passed through the hands of many powerful men close to the Crown. This large estate remains a home, so the house is full of family portraits, heirlooms and treasures.

The stunning grounds are twice yearly used as the site for the Weald of Kent Craft Fair, which allows talented craftspeople to exhibit and sell their work. Everything from leather tankards to delicate silverware helps to make this a varied and popular event and enables Penshurst to remain a sociable and active stately home.

Chiddingstone Castle

A consistent problem with large privately owned properties and estates is the constant drain on capital required for maintenance. Chiddingstone Castle is a case in point. Henry Streatfeild took over the property, his ancestral home, at the beginning of the nineteenth century and began work on it, restyling and extending it in the fashionable neo-Gothic style of the period. Unfortunately he ran out of funds and it was left to his son to complete his vision. The grand ambitions for the castle eventually became too heavy a burden for the Streatfeild family, and in the 1930s they decided that they could no longer afford the upkeep of the house.

The castle was without an owner for about twenty years. In 1955, however, Denys Bower recognised the potential of Chiddingstone and purchased it. He was a passionate collector of antiques, and he filled the castle with his possessions. Despite Bower's enthusiasm, he too found the upkeep too expensive. On his death in 1977 the property transferred to and continues to be maintained by a charitable trust, the Denys Eyre Bower Bequest, which has transformed the castle into a lively and exciting place for people to visit and share in the dream of a nobleman's home.

Hever Castle

An initial question for many people on their first visit to Hever Castle is why is the Tudor home of Anne Boleyn, Henry VIII's second wife, surrounded by Italian renaissance garden sculpture? This vision was created by American millionaire William Waldorf Astor, of salad and hotel fame.

This magnificent castle dates from the latter part of the thirteenth century. However, it is best known as the home of the Bullen (Boleyn) family who modernised and established it as their home in the early sixteenth century. After a time in France, Anne Boleyn returned to Hever Castle before becoming lady-in-waiting to Catherine of Aragon, catching the king's eye and sealing her fate.

Several families owned the castle over the centuries until 1903, when Astor purchased the property. Astor's love of Italy stemmed from a period as the United States' Ambassador there; the loggia fountain echoes that of the Trevi in Rome. Despite this recent Italian influence, the extensive grounds of Hever Castle also offer a variety of wonders, including a Tudor garden, a yew hedge maze and a staggering 360ft long herbaceous border.

Even today as you stroll through the castle you sense the whispers of Anne Boleyn's love affair and catch glimpses of an American's dream. This place has provided a happy home for centuries.

Chartwell

Although best known as the home of Winston Churchill and his family, Chartwell is also a beautiful place to visit, enjoying stunning views from its magnificent position in the Weald of Kent.

The interior of the house has been preserved to reflect Churchill's life, incorporating elements of both the politician and the artist. But before you reach the house itself you are guided along pathways lined with almost tropical-looking plants, out into the open to see a tranquil lake and then across a grassy bank dotted with apple trees. The landscape would have provided Churchill with a peace and solace much needed after the demands of Government life.

As well as making a magnificent contribution to literature (which earned him the Nobel Prize for Literature in 1953), Churchill was a keen and accomplished painter. It is in the grounds of Chartwell that he created a studio in which he painted many of his 500 or so works, several of which are on permanent display.

Emmett's Garden

The great storm of October 1987 destroyed a large part of Kent's woodland and forest, and, standing at 600ft on a sandstone ridge, Emmett's Garden was by no means an exception.

The 4-acre garden and arboretum and 14-acre wooded valley underwent an extensive replanting programme, using many of the species of exotic and rare trees and shrubs that were planted when the gardens were originally created between 1893 and 1895. The devastation swept away a precious part of the Kentish countryside, but it left a clearing where visitors can stand at one of the highest points in the county and enjoy a spectacular panoramic view of the Kentish Weald.

Squerryes Court

Squerryes Court has been in the Warde family since 1731, when it was purchased by John Warde from his friend, the 3rd Earl of Jersey. This seventeenth-century manor sits in a stunning landscape and has formal gardens, an impressive lake and woodlands which are ideal for walking.

Over the years the family has amassed a large collection of sixteenth- and seventeenth-century paintings, ceramics and other antiques, such as tapestries and furniture. There is an overwhelming sense of homeliness in this warm and inviting place and it is for this reason that so many people travel to visit this grand English manor.

Quebec House

James Wolfe only lived at Quebec House for the first eleven years of his life, so it is a testament to his achievements and reputation that this building receives a constant flow of visitors. General Wolfe successfully led his forces against the French in the Battle for Quebec in 1759, during the Seven Years War. However, he was mortally wounded during the siege and the province of Quebec became both his prize and his deathbed.

The house itself began life as Spiers, but the name was changed to Quebec when Wolfe became a national hero. In addition to its historical connections, it is a building of much interest in its own right. It has significant architectural features that show its sixteenth-century origins and the many changes and developments since then.

Eynsford Castle

Today all that remains of Eynsford Castle are 30ft sections of the curved wall and some internal features. The building is over 900 years old and is one of the earliest stone castles built in England.

It began its life on a manmade site next to the River Darent that had been used during Saxon times, and over the decades coursed flint walls were built up to provide strength. Much of the castle was destroyed by fire, and it was rebuilt and extended by William de Eynsford in the thirteenth century into a much larger and more comfortable home. The castle sits a short walk from the village of Eynsford, which is an example of a timeless Kentish village with pubs and tea rooms, and in the summer months children paddling and fishing in the shallows of the river – while the modern world passes it by.

Lullingstone Roman Villa

The ancient world was a period of discovery and enlightenment. The Egyptians are well known for having established various forms of communication and Rome continued to develop art, literature and symbolism. Indeed, one of the best examples of such art and symbolism was in their homes, where ornaments, glass and mosaics displayed a breathtaking quality of craftsmanship.

The 'Rape of Europa by Jupiter' is an extraordinary mosaic in what would have been the dining room of this first-century building in Lullingstone, one of the best preserved Roman villas in this country. It was located in what was a very prosperous part of Roman Britain until the end of the Roman occupation in 410 AD.

The discovery of the villa coincided with the outbreak of the Second World War, so excavations were postponed until 1949. The remains of the villa are preserved in a covered building and are complemented by a display of objects uncovered at the site. This location is considered to be one of the most exciting archaeological finds in England.

Down House

Charles Darwin's life was an extraordinary journey of discovery; he experienced both joy and pain in his professional and personal life. A five-year voyage around the world that began in 1831 was a pivotal event for him, but it also exposed him to numerous illnesses that plagued him for the rest of his life. The specimens he collected started off a chain reaction of discoveries and opinions which he presented to the scientific world.

It was, of course, Darwin's theory of evolution, published in *On The Origin Of Species* in 1859 and its description of 'the survival of the fittest', for which he became best known.

Down House was a family home as well as a place of study. The grounds provided Darwin with inspiration and time to formulate his ideas, but the property required considerable enlargement when it was first purchased. Darwin also extended the land, buying plots from his neighbours.

It is remarkable how the efforts of this one man changed the way people thought at the time and how his theories and influences are still being recognised to this day.

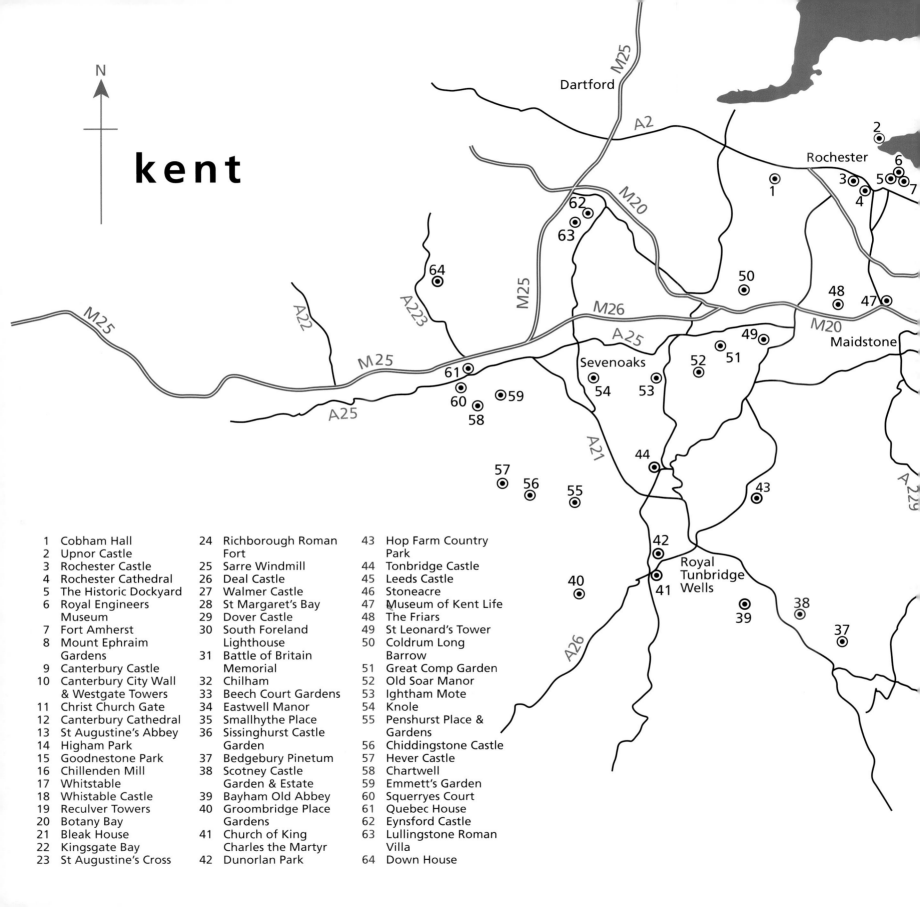

kent

N

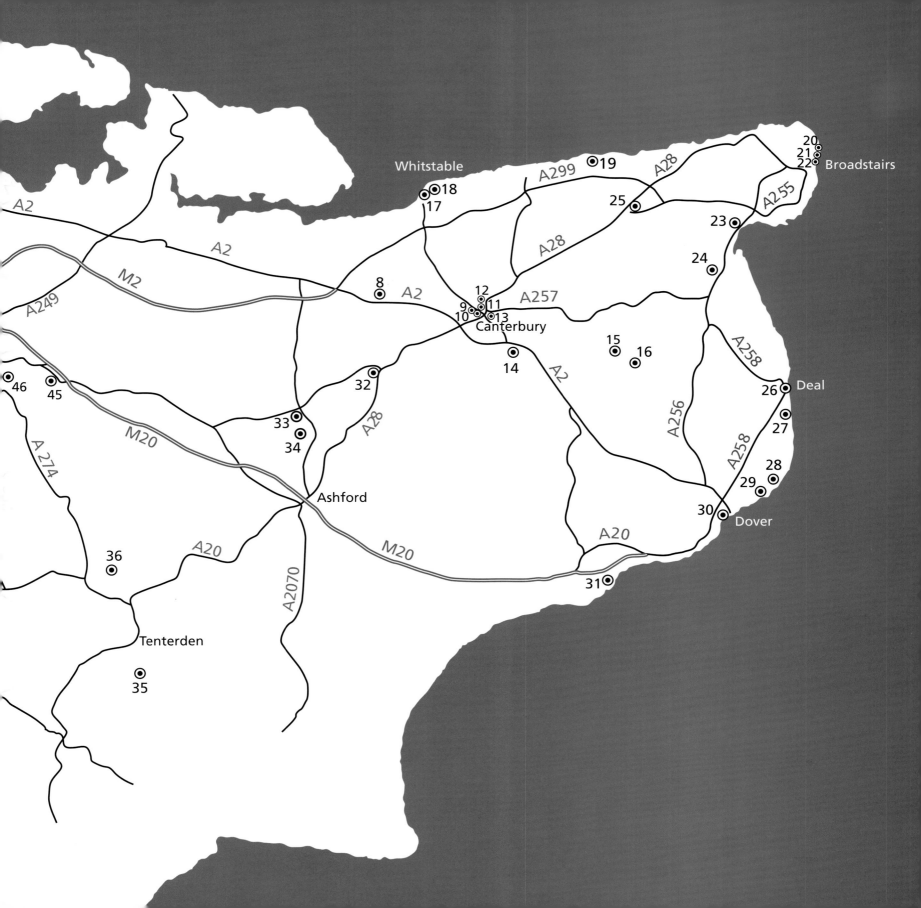

locations & contact details

historic **kent**

Cobham Hall

Cobham
Kent
DA12 3BL
01474 823371
www.cobhamhall.com

Upnor Castle

High Street
Upper Upnor
Rochester
Kent
ME2 4XG
01634 718742
www.medway.gov.uk/tourism
email: visitor.centre@medway.gov.uk

Rochester Castle

The Keep
Castle Hill
Rochester
Kent
ME1 1SW
01634 402276
www.medway.gov.uk/tourism
email: visitor.centre@medway.gov.uk

Rochester Cathedral

The Precinct
Rochester
Kent
ME1 1SX
01634 401301
email: visitsofficer@rochestercathedraluk.org
www.rochestercathedral.org

The Historic Dockyard

Chatham
Kent
ME4 4TZ
01634 823800
01634 823807
email: info@chdt.org.uk
www.thedockyard.co.uk

Royal Engineers Museum

Brompton Barracks
Chatham
Kent
ME4 4UG
01634 822839

Fort Amherst

Dock Road
Chatham
Kent
ME4 4UB
01634 847747
www.fortamherst.com
email: info@fortamherst.com

Mount Ephraim Gardens

Hernhill
Faversham
Kent
ME13 9TX
01227 751496
fax: 01227 750940
www.mountephraimgardens.co.uk

Canterbury Castle

Gas Street
Canterbury
Kent
www.canterbury.co.uk

City Wall & Westgate Towers

St Peter's Street
Canterbury
Kent
www.canterbury-museums.co.uk

Christ Church Gate

www.canterbury-cathedral.org
email: enquiries@canterbury-cathedral.org

Canterbury Cathedral

The Precinct
Canterbury
Kent
CT1 2EH
01227 762862
www.canterbury-cathedral.org
email: enquiries@canterbury-cathedral.org

St Augustine's Abbey

Longport
Canterbury
Kent
CT1 1TF
01227 767345
www.english-heritage.org.uk

Goodnestone Park Gardens

Wingham
Canterbury
Kent
CT3 1PL
01304 840107
www.goodnestoneparkgardens.co.uk

Chillenden Mill

Chillenden
Canterbury
Kent
CT3 1PR

Whitstable Castle

Tower Hill
Whitstable
Kent

Reculver Towers

www.english-heritage.org.uk

Botany Bay

www.tourism.thanet.gov.uk
www.thanet.gov.uk
01843 577644

Bleak House

www.bleakhouse.biz

Kingsgate Bay

www.tourism.thanet.gov.uk
www.thanet.gov.uk
01843 577644

St Augustine's Cross

www.english-heritage.org.uk

Richborough Roman Fort

Richborough Road
Sandwich
Kent
CT13 9JW
01304 612013
www.english-heritage.org.uk

Sarre Windmill

Ramsgate Road
Sarre
Nr Birchington
Kent
CT7 0JU
01843 847573

Deal Castle

Victoria Road
Deal
Kent
CT14 7BA
01304 372762
www.english-heritage.org.uk

Walmer Castle & Gardens

Kingsdown Road
Deal
Kent
CT14 7LJ
01304 364288
www.english-heritage.org.uk

St Margaret's Bay

Station Road
St Margaret's-at-Cliffe
Dover
Kent
01304 853990 (parish office)

Dover Castle

Castle Hill
Dover
Kent
CT16 1HU
01304 211067
www.english-heritage.org.uk

South Foreland Lighthouse

The Front
St Margaret's Bay
Dover
Kent
CT15 6HP
01304 852463
email: southforeland@nationaltrust.org.uk

Battle of Britain Memorial

Capel-le-Ferne
Folkestone
Kent
CT18 7JJ
01303 249292

Beech Court Gardens

Challock
Ashford
Kent
TN25 4DJ
01233 740735
www.beechcourtgardens.co.uk

Eastwell Manor Hotel

Eastwell Park
Boughton Lees
Ashford
Kent
TN25 4HR
01233 213000
fax 01233 635530
email: enquiries@eastwellmanor.co.uk
www.eastwellmanor.co.uk

Smallhythe Place

Smallhythe
Tenterden
Kent
TN30 7NG
01580 762334
www.nationaltrust.org.uk

Sissinghurst Castle Garden

Biddenden Road
Cranbrook
Kent
TN17 2AB
01580 710700
www.nationaltrust.org.uk/sissinghurst

Bedgebury Pinetum

Park Lane
Goudhurst
Cranbrook
Kent
TN17 2SL
01580 211044
www.forestry.gov.uk/bedgebury
www.bedgeburypinetum.org.uk

Scotney Castle Garden & Estate

Lamberhurst
Tunbridge Wells
Kent
TN3 8JN
01892 891081
www.nationaltrust.org.uk/scotneycastle

Bayham Old Abbey

Lamberhurst
Kent
TN3 8DE
0870 3331181
www.english-heritage.org.uk

Groombridge Place Gardens

Groombridge
Tunbridge Wells
Kent
TN3 9QG
01892 861444
www.groombridge.co.uk

Church of King Charles the Martyr

King Charles Parish Office
King Charles Hall
3 Warwick Park
Tunbridge Wells
Kent
TN2 5TA
01892 511745
www.kcmtw.org
email: kingcharlesthemartyr@hotmail.com

Dunorlan Park

Pembury Road
Royal Tunbridge Wells
Kent
TN2 3QA
01892 526121
www.tunbridgewells.gov.uk/dunorlan

The Hop Farm Country Park

Paddock Wood
Kent
TN12 6PY
01622 872068
www.thehopfarm.co.uk

Tonbridge Castle

Tonbridge
Kent
TN9 1BG
01732 770929
www.tonbridgecastle.org

Leeds Castle

Maidstone
Kent
ME17 1PL
01622 765400
www.leeds-castle.com

Stoneacre

Stoneacre Lane
Otham
Maidstone
Kent
ME15 8RS
01622 862157
www.nationaltrust.org.ug
email: stoneacrent@aol.com

Museum of Kent Life

Lock Lane
Sandling
Maidstone
Kent
ME14 3AU
01622 763936
www.museum-kentlife.co.uk
email: enquiries@museum-kentlife.co.uk

The Friars

Aylesford
Kent
ME20 7BX
01622 717272
email: enquiry@thefriars.org.uk
www.thefriars.org.uk

St Leonard's Tower

West Malling
Kent
www.english-heritage.org.uk

Coldrum Long Barrow

(off) Pinesfield Lane
Trottiscliffe
Kent
ME19 5EL
www.nationaltrust.org.uk

Great Comp Garden

St Mary's Platt
Borough Green
Kent
TN15 8QS
01732 886154
www.greatcomp.co.uk

Old Soar Manor

The National Trust
Old Soar Lane
Plaxtol
Borough Green
Kent
TN15 0QX
01732 810378
www.nationaltrust.org.uk/oldsoarmanor

Ightham Mote

The National Trust
Ightham Mote
Mote Road
Ivy Hatch
Sevenoaks
Kent
TN15 0NT
01732 811145
www.nationaltrust.org.uk/ighthammote

Knole

Sevenoaks
Kent
TN15 0RP
01732 462100
www.nationaltrust.org.uk

Penshurst Place

Penshurst
Tonbridge
Kent
TN11 8DG
01892 870307
www.penshurstplace.com

Chiddingstone Castle

Chiddingstone
near Edenbridge
Kent
TN8 7AD
01892 870347
email: chiddingstonecastle@yahoo.co.uk
www.chiddingstone-castle.org.uk

Hever Castle

Hever
Edenbridge
Kent
TN8 7NG
01732 865224
email: mail@hevercastle.co.uk
www.hevercastle.co.uk

Chartwell

Westerham
Kent
TN16 1PS
01732 866368
www.nationaltrust.org.uk

Emmett's Garden

Ide Hill
Sevenoaks
Kent
TN14 6AY
01732 750367
www.nationaltrust.org.uk

Squerryes Court

Westerham
Kent
TN16 1SJ
01959 562345
www.squerryes.co.uk
email: squerryes.court@squerryes.co.uk

Quebec House

Quebec Square
Westerham
TN16 1TD
01959 562206
www.nationaltrust.org.uk

Eynsford Castle

Eynsford
Kent
DA44 0AA
0870 333 1183
www.english-heritage.org.uk

Lullingstone Roman Villa

Lullingstone Lane
Eynsford
Kent
DA4 0JA
01322 863467
www.english-heritage.org.uk

Down House

The Home of Charles Darwin
Luxted Road
Downe
Kent
BR6 7JT
01689 859119
www.english-heritage.org.uk

index

historic **kent**